CONTEMPORARY HANDMADE

TURKISH CARPETS

UĞUR AYYILDIZ
Art Historian and Professional Guide

NET®
TURİSTİK YAYINLAR
SANAYİ VE TİCARET A.Ş.

All carpets in this book are part of the Bazaar 54 collection.

Published and distributed by:
NET TURİSTİK YAYINLAR A.Ş.

Şifa Hamamı Sok. No. 18/2, 34400 Sultanahmet-İstanbul/Turkey
Tel: (90-212) 516 32 28 - 516 84 67 34 Fax: (90-212) 516 84 68

236. Sokak No.96/B Funda Apt., 35360 Hatay/İzmir/Turkey
Tel: (90-232) 228 78 51 Fax: (232-51) 250 22 73

Kışla Mah., 54. Sok., İlteray Apt., No.11/A-B, 07040 Antalya/Turkey
Tel: (90-242) 248 93 67 - 243 14 97 Fax: (90-242) 248 93 68

Eski Kayseri Cad., Dirikoçlar Apt. No.45, 50200 Nevşehir/Turkey
Tel: (90-384) 213 30 89 - 213 46 20 Fax: (90-384) 213 40 36

Text: **Uğur Ayyıldız**
Translation: **Nüket Eraslan**
Photographs: **Net Archiv**
Layout: **Not Ajans**
Typesetting: **AS&64 Ltd. Şti.**
Colour separation: **Mas Matbaacılık A.Ş.**
Printed in Turkey by: **Mas Matbaacılık A.Ş.**

ISBN 975-479-146-5

3rd Edition, 1995

CONTENTS

PREFACE

Precious handmade carpets are the products of long months of labour, requiring great skill and patience. Besides being utilitarian objects, they are a source of pleasure to their owners.

A beautiful carpet is like a fine painting; it pleases the eye. It is also an investment which will retain its value as the years pass.

Contemporary Turkish carpets are made by local experts who use materials and designs characteristic of the region in which they work. After a quality inspection and a first washing, these carpets enter the domestic and foreign markets through well known dealers.

The second half of the 20th century is another golden era of Turkish handmade carpet production, due to the making of high quality carpets displaying new designs, and it coincides with the period when Turkey is a popular holiday destination with tourists.

In the main centres of tourism and along the roads connecting them, many carpet stores, production and sales centres have been established. Original handmade carpets, sold where they are produced, have become very popular with customers. Famous companies that offer a great variety of carpets of different sizes and designs, with a guarantee of authenticity, are contributing to the increase in carpet sales. Handmade Turkish carpets are one of the main export items of Turkey and they are shipped all over the world.

This catalogue is an illustrated guide to comtemporary Turkish carpets, region by region.

INTRODUCTION

Until recently, all artifacts had to be handmade, but modern technology and mass production have replaced skill and techniques traditional for thousands of years.

Today, handmade works are rare, and among them are the beautiful and functional knotted carpets made by using traditional methods which have developed over a period of more than 2000 years.

Carpets are textile products. Turkish handmade carpets have always had patterns suitable for the specific nature of the materials and the knotting used. Another special characteristic of Turkish handmade carpets is the use of the double knot, known as the Turkish or Gördes knot. Although designs and patterns change and diversify, the Turkish carpet always retains its historical and traditional features.

Carpet weaving is collective work using skills passed on for generations. Families, tribes, or even whole villages work collectively, pooling their special skills, knowledge and expertise. The various methods of weaving and the different raw materials used, produce distinctive carpets, characteristic of the region in which they are woven.

Handmade knotted carpets are used for various purposes by the local people in their region of origin. Besides being used as rugs, carpets serve as tent screens, paintings, cradle and sofa covers, wall hangings and prayer rugs.

A beautiful high quality handmade carpet increases in value as it is used; for the carpet's knots tighten, making it more brilliant and valuable.

According to taste and tradition, Turkish handmade carpets may be used in every room of a house, as well as in hotels, either spread on the floor or hung on a wall.

A high quality handmade carpet, carefully selected, is an attractive decorative object which is passed down from generation to generation. A handmade carpet, used either as a rug or a wall hanging, is always complementary to the rare and valuable objects of art with which it is found. On the other hand, it is possible to tastefully decorate even simple rooms using either small or large carpets, with floral or geometric designs in brilliant or pastel colours. No matter what purpose they serve, with their beatiful designs and colours, handmade carpets create a pleasing and cosy atmosphere in the rooms in which they are used.

The owners and admirers of such carpets may not realise that these works of art are rare creations of anonymous artisans. A high quality carpet, on which the children play and other members of the family take pleasure in seeing, is a necessary and valuable household item.

Turkish handmade carpets are items sought after in the region in which they are produced, in the western world, and in the oil-producing countries of the Middle East.

International carpet markets are amazed with the achievements and progress seen today in Turkish handmade carpet production.

Besides the standard quality carpets produced in different regions in Turkey, there are better quality, tighter-knotted carpets woven by using the same kind of material and motifs.

Carpet-weaving loom.

THE STORY OF CARPETS

HISTORY

Private collectors, distinguished families and museums are proud owners of antique carpets. The richest collections of antique, knotted handmade carpets are found in the Istanbul Museum of Turkish and Islamic Arts, the Vakıf Carpet Museum in the Blue Mosque, and the Konya Mevlana Museum. The museums and collectors of Europe and the USA own some exquisite pieces, most of which have been exported from Turkey. During the 14th, 15th and 16th centuries, handmade Turkish carpets were prized possessions of the noble and wealthy families of Europe. Surviving carpets of this era, are now on display in museums.

For the last century or more, handmade knotted carpets have been a subject of research for experts and art historians. Great numbers of books and journals have been published on the subject, showing that the making of handmade carpets is an important art form. The spread of knowledge through such publications has caused an increased demand for fine carpets.

Carpets are produced in an area extending from the Mediterranean coast of Turkey to the steppes of Central Asia, and authorities conclude that the art of weaving knotted carpets, was introduced by Turkish nomadic tribes and craftsmen. Traditional Turkish carpet making with its distinctive techniques, materials, patterns and knotting, has had a strong influence upon all oriental carpets. In art history books, one comes across carpets that date back to the Pharaohs, the ancient Persians and the Caliphs. However, these were not knotted carpets, but were rugs woven using the simple "towel" technique.

The hard-wearing, double-knotted carpets are the invention of Turkish tribes. The techniques used in handmade carpets were brought to the Mediterranean coast by the Seljuks in the 12th century. Marco Polo mentions rich displays of carpets in palaces and mosques. The demand for carpets in different periods dictated the pace of the development of carpet weaving, but high quality handmade carpets have always found a ready market.

Textile products are not resistant to destruction by nature. The oldest carpet known was discovered, frozen in ice, by Russian archaeologists in 1984, and it is called the "Pazırık" carpet. This carpet, which measures 1.80 m by 2 m., is dated to the 4th-1st centuries B.C. and is on exhibit in the Her-

Animal-figured carpet late 15th c., exhibited at the Carpet Museum, İstanbul.

mitage in St. Petersburg (Leningrad). The "Pazırık" carpet is tightly knotted, and therefore indicates that the art of carpet weaving had emerged long before its production. Discovered in the mausoleum of the leader of a migratory tribe, who lived in the region and during the age of the Turkish Huns, the "Pazırık" carpet is an early and the sole example exhibiting the Turkish double knot. Not much is known of the progress of the art of knotted carpet weaving prior to the Seljuk Turkish Empire (11th century A.D.)

Some of the pieces of carpets discovered in Turkmenistan, and dating to the 3rd-6th centuries A.D., are in museums.

Development of the Turkish art of carpet weaving since the 12th century is known. Besides the carpets themselves, in Turkey and other countries, it is possible to see examples of Turkish carpets in the paintings of 15th-16th century European painters.

In general, the Seljuk carpets have geometric designs. Starting in the 15th century, the Ottoman carpets were imported to Europe by Latin traders, and thus elegant, durable and decorative carpets were used in the western world for the first time.

The stylised animal figures and geometric designs used in the 14th and 15th centuries were replaced by stylised plant motifs in the 16th century. The 17th century is the age of Ottoman Imperial carpets with designs of medallions and detailed plant motifs. Rooted traditions ensured the progress of the art of carpet weaving even during the difficult periods in the Ottoman Empire.

General wiev of the carpet Museum, İstanbul.

Milas prayer rug, 19th c., exhibited at the Carpet Museum, İstanbul.

The silk carpets produced on the palace-subsidised looms of Hereke and Kumkapı in the 19th century, are amazingly beautiful museum pieces. After 1923, and Turkey becoming a Republic, the State subsidised the production of carpets from time to time.

In regard to variety, quality and price, today's Turkish handmade carpets, produced in both private and State-subsidised workshops, along with those produced in towns and villages, are durable and beautiful handmade products popular all over the world.

DESIGN, MATERIAL AND TECHNIQUE

The carpets shown in this book are knotted handmade rugs woven mostly by women.

The first step in carpet weaving is to decide on a design or a motif. In regional carpet production, experienced weavers create the design as they weave, whereas in the production of tight-knotted carpets a pattern to refer to is necessary.

"Sümerbank", a State owned company, after long years of research and labour, has successfully re-introduced almost all of the designs of old Turkish carpets to the carpet market, but with a modern approach and new concepts. Leading companies too, through their own efforts, produce new motifs derived from the old ones. There is a great variety of motifs of geometric designs. Stylised animal, human and plant motifs are found scattered among the geometric designs, and the colours used bring out these motifs.

Some of the carpets with floral designs exhibit such harmony and colours that they resemble flower gardens. The carnival of flowers, branches and plants that covers the surface of the carpets is always framed by a complementing design.

The most important element in design is proportion. The design should be weaved in such a manner that there should be no irregularities in the corners.

The carpets with a "mihrab" design (seccade) may have different designs in or around the "mihrab", and decorations of Arabic letters may be seen in the borders.

The design is drawn in sections on sheets of millimetric paper and placed on the loom to help the weaver. As the carpet increases in size, the number of these sections increase too.

The second most important element is the material used, which varies according to the type of carpet. It may be wool, pure silk, cotton or mercerised, or silk-like cotton called floss.

Bursa is one of the few centres of silk production in the world, and for centuries, the pure silk produced here has been used in the making of handmade Turkish carpets. The real beauty of silk comes out best of all in these

Drying newly dyed wool.

magnificent looking rugs and wall carpets. Lamb's wool is the most popular material used. The grasslands of the Anatolian plateaux are the reason behind the durability and sheen of the wool. Turkey is a land of sheep and lambs, and therefore wool is plentiful. The wool used in carpet production must be special: strong and soft. In certain regions, the wool, as in the old days, is spun by hand to make the yarn used in carpet weaving. Today, textiles are a major industry in Turkey, and the country is a leading cotton producer.

In carpet weaving, the base (warp and weft) is constructed of cotton; wool is then knotted onto this to form the pile. Such handmade carpets made of both cotton and wool, are as attractive and durable as the others. Floss is used only in Kayseri carpets, and it makes up thepile. As floss is easily dyed, bright and attractive carpets in a variety of colours are produced by using floss.

Knotted carpets are woven on a loom consisting of horizontal bars, onto which the warp threads are stretched. Onto these threads, the pile knots are tied according to the pattern. The thread ends, which make up the pile, are clipped off to get a velvet-like soft surface. Thus, the motifs are made up of thousands of individual knots. The tighter the knots, the finer and

Some of the motifs used in the designs of Turkish handmade carpets.

Ram Horn: Symbol of power.

Cypress: Symbol of eternity and tree of life.

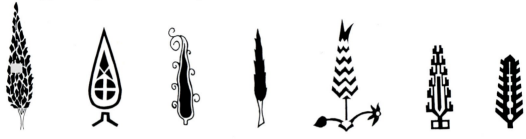

Wheel of Fortune: Symbol of fate.

Chest: Symbol of a maiden's trousseau.

Grain: Symbol of abundance.

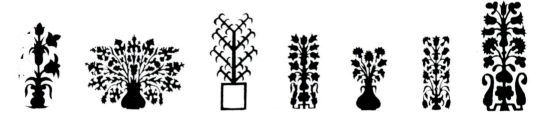

Eye: A motif used to keep the evil away.

Scorpion: Symbol of pride and liberty.

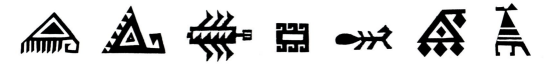

Head band: Symbol of wish for matrimony.

Akimbo: Symbol of motherhood. Also symbolises the lady who has woven the carpet.

Birds in flight: Symbol of good news.

Lovebird: Symbol of love.

Ear of grain: Symbol of birth and fertility.

stronger is the carpet. The pleasure one gets from a beautiful carpet equals the pleasure one gets from a beautiful painting.

The double knot, known as the Turkish or Gördes knot, is used in all typical Turkish carpets. Another well known system is the Sehna or Persian knot. The Turkish knot is wrapped around two warps and the Persian knot around a single warp. A kilim, which is similar to a carpet, is woven on the loom but with a different technique; knots are not used.

The Gördes knot makes a carpet stronger, firmer and more durable, while the Sehna knot allows the weaving of different patterns. However, once a carpet is made it is difficult to determine the knotting system used.

Dyeing wool.

Above, the strong Turkish double-Knot, and below, the Iranian single-knot.

The colours also are characteristic of the region where the carpet is made. The threads used in the weaving of antique carpets used to be dyed with natural dyes, the formulas of which were known only by the family that manufactured the carpet. Today, chemical dyes are used along with vegetal dyes. Natural dyes are produced from leaves, roots, and fruits. Many of the villages engaged in carpet making have a grazing land called "Boyalık". Plants from which dyes are made are grown there. The various formulas for dye production have been passed down from generation to generation. Thus the colours traditional to Turkish carpet production have survived till today. Red is dominant in Turkish carpets. This striking colour expresses wealth, joy and happiness. Green symbolises heaven; blue nobility and grandeur; yellow is believed to keep evil away, and black symbolises purification from worries.

Handmade carpets are generally called after the region or town where they are produced. Contemporary carpets are made in various sizes and with combinations of different materials. In some regions, the threads used in weaving and the knots may be only wool, and in other regions, the base may be cotton and the knots wool. In still other regions pure silk is used in the weaving of carpets.

Besigning and Technique using special tools.

DIMENSIONS AND NOMENCLATURE

Handmade carpets that can be used as rugs, wall hangings and divan covers are manufactured in various sizes. Different names are given to carpets of different sizes. Although the names given according to size are the same for all regions, the carpets, because they are handmade, may show minor differences in dimension. While some regions manufacture carpets of all sizes, others manufacture carpets in standard sizes. Whatever the size is, a handmade carpet adds beauty and elegance to the place where it is used. Two or three handmade carpets laid over wall-to-wall carpeting will add colour to the rooms.

Standard dimensions in centimetres:	
Small yastık (pillow)	40×25
Yastık	100×60
Çeyrek	135×90
Seccade (prayer rug)	180×120 - 200×130
Karyola	220×150
Kelle	300×200
Taban	over 6 sq. metres
Yolluk (runner)	different sizes

CARE OF A CARPET

Handmade carpets are used either as rugs or wall hangings. To preserve their beauty and durability, constant care is necessary. In order to control the bleeding of the colours later, quality carpets are marketed after a special washing.

The pile attracts dust and dirt, therefore, regular cleaning is required to keep the carpets bright and attractive. Vacuum cleaners used in homes, are ideal for cleaning handmade carpets as they suck away the dust and dirt Carpets which have not been cleaned properly for many years should be sent to professional carpet cleaners.

Handmade carpets should not be cleaned like machine made, wall-to-wall carpets. Moisture, grease and moths are the enemies of carpets. Wet carpets should be dried immediately in shade. From time to time, carpets may be wiped with a damp sponge or a white piece of cloth dipped in soapy water, in the same direction. Care must be taken not to get the underside of the carpet wet. A hairdryer may be used to dry damp carpets. Handmade carpets are a part of everyday life and naturally, they are used a lot. When not used for a certain period of time, they should be rolled with moth balls, wrapped in a piece of cloth and stored in a dry place. Worn-out fringes may be replaced in time. Carpets should be repaired by experts only.

CARPET WEAVING CENTRES

Technically, Turkish handmade carpets may be classified as Anatolian carpets. The carpets produced in towns and villages, and by the ''Yörük'' nomads, reflect their art tradition. However, the personal feelings and taste of the weaver may be reflected along with the traditional patterns. The sale of handmade carpets contributes a lot to the income of the family. Almost every region of Anatolia still produces great numbers of handmade carpets in traditional ways, making up beautiful collections. The village folk weave carpets characteristic of the region on the looms in their homes. Besides such local centres, carpet weaving has become an industry in certain cities and towns.

High quality handmade carpets are manufactured in homes, private workshops or in institutions subsidised by the government, and they display a rich variety of colour, design and size. The demand for handmade carpets can only be met by the production coming from these centres.

The carpet weaving centres and regions, as well as the different materials used in those centres are shown on the map overleaf.

HANDMAD...
WEAVING...
OF TU...

BULGARIA

GREECE

EDİRNE

KIRKLARELİ

TEKİRDAĞ

İSTANBUL

SEA OF MARMARA

İZMİT

Hereke

BOLU

ZONGULDAK

KASTAMONU

BL...

SİNO...

ÇANKIRI

ÇOR...

ADAPAZARI

ÇANAKKALE

BURSA

BİLECİK

Ezine

Edremit

Bursa

ESKİŞEHİR

ANKARA

KIRŞEHİR

YOZGAT

BALIKESİR

Bergama

KÜTAHYA

KIRŞEHİR

MANİSA

Gördes

Kula

UŞAK

AFYON

Taşpınar

NEVŞEHİR

İZMİR

Başmakçı

Ladik

AKSARAY

NİĞD...

AYDIN

DENİZLİ

KONYA

Milas

MUĞLA

ISPARTA

BURDUR

Döşemealtı

Şirvan

Niğde-Kars

KARAMAN

MERSİN

ANTALYA

AEGEAN SEA

MEDITERRANEAN SEA

T.R.N.C.

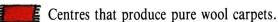 Centres that produce pure wool carpets.

Centres that produce pure silk carpets.

SEA

RUSSIA

GEORGIA

ARMENIA

AZERBAYCAN

NAHCIVAN

IRAN

IRAQ

SYRIA

SAMSUN

ORDU

GIRESUN

TRABZON

RIZE

ARTVIN

ARDAHAN

KARS

Kars

MASYA

TOKAT

GÜMÜŞHANE

BAYBURT

AĞRI

IĞDIR

Sivas

SIVAS

ERZINCAN

ERZURUM

TUNCELI

BINGÖL

MUŞ

Bünyan

ELAZIĞ

BITLIS

VAN

Kayseri

MALATYA

SIIRT

HAKKARI

ıyalı

DIYARBAKIR

ADIYAMAN

Yörük

BATMAN

ŞIRNAK

örük

K.MARAŞ

Yörük

ANA

GAZIANTEP

Ş.URFA

MARDIN

ANTAKYA

FATIH

Centres that produce floss silk carpets.

Yörük (Nomadic) pure wool carpets producing regions.

BUYING A CARPET

Handmade Turkish carpets are useful, functional objects as well as investments for the future. When choosing among a wide range of exquisite carpets, the first criterion is falling in love at first sight. The carpet must fascinate and enrapture the buyer. However, quality is also very important, and that can vary greatly. A reputable and expert dealer carefully chooses beautiful high quality carpets and keeps an extensive stock.

Expensive, antique carpets are beyond the reach of many people, and difficult to find. Every old carpet is not considered an antique piece and is not a collector's item. Both the buyer and seller of such antique carpets must be well informed. Antique carpets are difficult to export, as well as hard to find and appraise.

For centuries, Turkish handmade carpets have been produced using the same techniques, the same designs and the same knotting system, and today, there are as many varieties as before. The carpets with the tightest knots, and displaying quality workmanship, are the most valuable. Similar carpets

Bazaar 54 carpet showroom.

Bazaar 54 carpet showrooms.

may differ in quality. Reputable firms neither produce, nor buy or sell loosely knotted, bulky carpets. Because of the high quality carpets marketed by such leading firms, the late 1900's has been another golden era for Turkish handmade carpets. A couple of generations later, contemporary high quality Turkish handmade carpets will be a valuable heirloom.

Even a single carpet, matching in colour with the other furnishings in a room, adds charm and creates a cosy atmosphere.

HEREKE

The most famous and finest pure silk carpets in the world are produced in the small town of Hereke, 60 km east of Istanbul. Pure silk carpets made here are unrivaled in value and quality.

Since the 19th century, Hereke has been one of the most important carpet weaving centres. The first looms were installed there upon the orders of the Sultan, for the making of carpets for the palace, the nobility, and important people. On these looms expert craftsmen of exceptional ability create valuable masterpieces full of charm. Naturalistic floral decoration is typical of the pure silk Hereke carpets. Plum blossoms, tulips, carnations, roses and other flowers create an atmosphere of spring. With a million knots per square metre, the natural silk Hereke carpets represent the supreme achievement in contemporary carpet weaving. Some of the carpets are brocaded in gold thread.

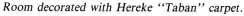

Room decorated with Hereke "Taban" carpet.

Hereke pure silk "Çeyrek" and prayer rugs.

Besides pure silk carpets made from the silk produced in Bursa, Hereke is also famous for its wool carpets.

Natural silk carpets are manufactured in various sizes; they may be as small as a table mat, or big enough to be a tapestry. Hereke wool carpets on the other hand, are for use in living rooms, dining rooms and bedrooms.

Increase in demand has forced the production of these special carpets outside Hereke too. Different size carpets bearing Hereke designs are produced in other regions. Collectors' items referred to as "fine and super", have extraordinarily tight knots, and they are the highest quality and the most valuable carpets of all.

Hereke pure silk "Çeyrek" carpet.

Hereke pure silk ''Çeyrek'' carpets.

Hereke pure wool "Kelle" carpets.

Hereke pure wool "Kelle" carpet.

Hereke pure wool on cotton prayer rugs.

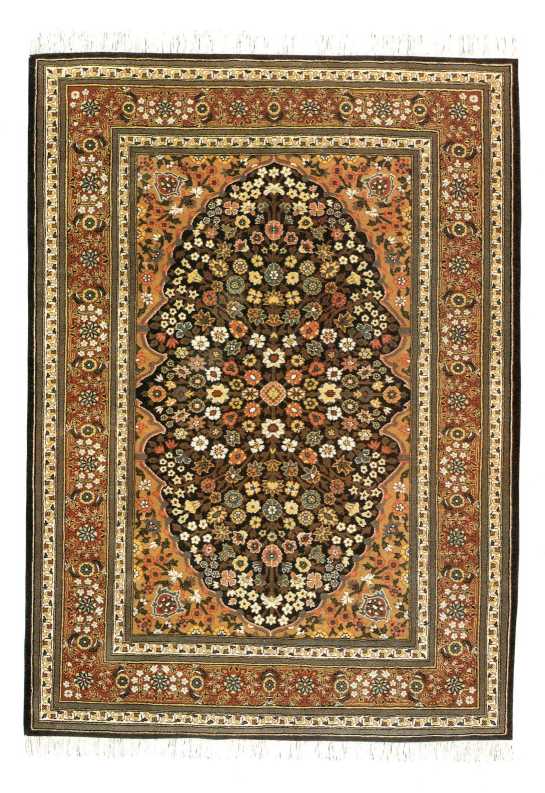

Hereke pure wool on cotton prayer rug.

KAYSERİ

The town of Kayseri, which is the capital of Cappadocia situated in Central Anatolia at the intersection of caravan roads and trade routes, is one of the most famous carpet manufacturing centres of Turkey. Here, carpets are produced using a variety of techniques and materials. The thousands of looms are an important source of income for the town itself and the nearby villages. Kayseri is the only centre where carpets of all sizes are manufactured. Kayseri and Hereke are world centres for best quality natural silk carpets. The carpets made with the natural silk produced in Bursa are very bright in colour and extremely decorative. Fine knotting and close pile make every detail of the design clearly visible. The same characteristics are found in the floss silk carpets produced in Kayseri. The handmade carpets produced using floss silk are very attractive and display excellent colour harmony. With their vary-

Room decorated with Kayseri floss silk carpet.

Kayseri Natural silk "Çeyrek" carpet.

ing sizes, they suit homes decorated in either classic or modern styles. These carpets adorned with traditional floral designs, fill the home with joy and create an atmosphere of a heavenly garden.

The Kayseri wool carpets produced in large sizes, are available in different colours and designs. Some Kayseri carpets are also known as "Bünyan" carpets, after a nearby town.

Kayseri naturel silk "Çeyrek" carpets.

Kayseri natural silk prayer rug.

Kayseri natural silk "Çeyrek" carpets

Kayseri floss silk runner.

Kayseri floss silk prayer rug.

Kayseri "Kelle" carpet.

Kayseri pure wool on cotton prayer rugs.

Kayseri pure wool on cotton "Karyola" carpet.

Kayseri pure wool on cotton prayer rugs

Kayseri "Taban" carpet with cotton base and wool knots.

BERGAMA

Bergama is one of the most famous ancient carpet weaving centres. Pure wool carpets of this region still retain the tradition of ages. Geometric patterns, red colour and limited standard sizes, are features of Bergama carpets.

Bergama pure wool carpet.

Bergama pure wool carpet.

YAĞCI BEDİR

The pure wool Yağcı Bedir carpets produced in the mountain villages of the Aegean region, are some of the best quality of their kind. The dominant colours of these very soft carpets are dark blue and red. The deep blue of the Aegean gives the basic colour. They are patterned with geometric forms, stylised birds and numerous stars of Solomon, and framed in a border of five or seven bands.

The warp, weft and knots of these carpets are made of pure lambswool. Due to the short clipped knots, the pattern is easily seen on the pile. These beautiful West Anatolian carpets are always produced in the same colours and patterns.

Bedroom decorated with Yağcıbedir pure wool carpet.

Yağcıbedir pure wool prayer rug.

Yağcıbedir pure wool prayer rugs.

Yağcıbedir pure wool runners.

Yağcıbedir pure wool "Kelle" carpet.

KULA

The production of handmade carpets in Western Anatolia and the Aegean region has a rich tradition and history. These carpets have been exported since the 16th century, and are generally known by the names of Kula or Izmir. They were used in churches and palaces. Sometimes one sees examples in the paintings of famous artists. Many of the classical, old hotels of the west were decorated with carpets from the Aegean region. The majority of the examples which have survived are considered to be rare pieces and are kept in museums.

Today, many carpet weaving centres outside the Aegean region produce pure wool carpets exhibiting the traditional Kula patterns. These carpets are the best examples of the Turkish art of carpet weaving and make one of the best souvenirs, since they can be handed down from generation to generation. They are manufactured in all sizes and colours.

Kula carpet decorating bar corner.

Kula pure wool "Karyola" carpet.

Kula pure wool prayer rugs.

Kula pure wool runners.

Kula pure wool "Karyola" carpet.

Kula pure wool "Çeyrek" carpets.

Kula pure wool "Çeyrek" carpet.

BAŞMAKÇI

These high quality carpets have designs of Caucassian origin and they are dyed with vegetal dyes. Soft and high-piled Başmakçı carpets are extremely decorative.

Başmakçı pure wool carpet.

Başmakçı pure wool carpet.

MİLAS

The Milas carpet, with its varied colours and compositions, has an important place in Western Anatolian carpet production.

Instead of the colours used in antique pieces, contemporary Milas carpets are made in pale, delicate tones produced with vegetal dyes.

The warp, weft and knots are pure wool. The dominant colors are yellow, the colour of tobacco, dark and light brown and reddish brown.

The geometric patterns which suit the production of pure wool carpets are the predominant design. Another characteristic feature is the use of the "mihrab" (prayer niche) pattern.

Milas carpets are manufactured in a limited range of sizes.

Room decorated with Milas wool carpet.

Milas pure wool "Karyola" carpet.

Milas pure wool prayer rugs.

Milas pure wool ''Kelle'' carpet.

Milas pure wool prayer rugs.

Milas pure wool "Kelle" carpet.

DÖŞEME ALTI

The Yürüks, who are semi-nomadic tribes, spend the winters on the warmer plains. They produce the handmade carpets called Döşemealtı, by using the pure wool and vegetal dyes they themselves make. The villages around Antalya and the Turkish Riviera, are the centre of this type of carpet making. The design reflects the nomadic taste, which is expressed in geometric patterns. and a colour harmony of blues, dark greens and reds.

Döşemealtı carpets are made in a limited range of sizes.

Room decorated with carpets from Döşemealtı and different regions.

Döşemealtı pure wool "Çeyrek" carpet.

Döşemealtı pure wool prayer rugs.

Döşemealtı pure wool runners.

Döşemealtı pure wool prayer rug.

Döşemealtı pure wool prayer rug.

CARPET WEAVING IN CENTRAL ANATOLIA

Volumes of books are required to describe all the carpets produced in the cities, towns and villages of Turkey. Volumes have already been written about antique Turkish carpets, but a similar number is required for contemporary Turkish carpets, therefore, only a few examples of each region have been mentioned. However, it should be noted that no photograph can reflect the actual brilliance, beauty and lustre of a handmade carpet. Kayseri, one of the main centres of this region, was mentioned in the previous pages. Carpets with different features and characteristics are manufactured in Kırşehir, Avanos, Ürgüp, Niğde, Maden and other centres. Sometimes the characteristics differ from one village to the next, which may be only a few kilometres away.

Winding wool.

YAHYALI

Yahyalı carpets are produced in a very small region. Pure wool and vegetal dyes are used in the making of Yahyalı carpets. These carpets, adorned with stylised floral patterns and geometric designs, are famous all over the world. Manufactured in villages, they reflect local colours and the use of high quality materials. The artists produce their own materials for weaving and dyeing. Dominant colours of a Yahyalı carpet are navy blue, red and brown; other colours are used among these. The major designs of a "mihrab" or a medallion are elaborated with the addition of geometric patterns. Yahyalı carpets are manufactured in a limited range of sizes.

Room decorated with Yahyalı wool carpet.

Yahyalı pure wool prayer rugs.

Yahyalı pure wool runner.

Yahyalı pure wool prayer rugs.

MADEN

These are also created by pure wool threads and vegetal dyes. The main colour is red, and designs are woven in soft colours. Geometric designs are enlivened with the addition of stylised floral patterns. The characteristic design is that of a medallion or a "mihrab". Maden carpets are manufactured in a limited range of sizes.

Maden pure wool "Seccade" carpet.

TAŞPINAR

Taşpınar carpets, made of high quality wool dyed with vegetal dyes, are manufactured in a small region. Yellow frames the centre of the carpet. Other dominant colours are bright red, navy or dark blue. The borders bearing geometric patterns, are enriched with the addition of stylised floral and rosette patterns. Taşpınar carpets are manufactured in a limited range of sizes.

Taşpınar pure wool prayer rug.

KONYA-LADİK

The oldest known carpet making centre in history is Konya. Marco Polo mentions the existence of workshops under the patronage of the Seljuk Sultans during the 13th century. Rare pieces from that century are exhibited in the carpet museums in Istanbul and Konya.

The Konya-Ladik carpets, with their high quality, varying sizes, soft colours and fine knotting, are rare pieces always in demand in the carpet markets of the world. The carpets manufactured in Konya and the nearby town of Ladik are copies of antique carpets.

Konya-Ladik carpets with their cotton base and wool knots are very popular, and suit tastes of all kinds. These carpets come in different sizes that can be used in living rooms and large spaces. Generally, natural dyes are used in the production of Konya-Ladik carpets. The dominant colours of these high quality carpets are mostly soft hues displayed in tasteful combinations.

Konya-Ladik "Taban" carpet, ideal for large room.

Konya-Ladik "Taban" carpet.

Konya-Ladik "Taban" carpets.

Konya-Ladik "Taban" carpet.

Konya-Ladik "Taban" carpet.

KONYA-ŞİRVAN

These are high quality carpets bearing geometric designs of Caucassian origin. They are made of handspun wool yarn in striking colours and pastels used together.

Konya-Şirvan pure wool carpet.

Konya-Şirvan pure wool carpet.

NİĞDE-KARS

The motifs of Kars and other Eastern Anatolian centres are used in the carpets produced in Niğde. Different colours, especially pastels, are the characteristics of these high-piled carpets. Compared to the carpets produced in other regions, these carpets do not have such tight knots.

Niğde-Kars pure wool "Karyola" carpet.

Niğde-Kars pure wool "Seccade" carpets.

Niğde-Kars pure wool "Karyola" carpet.

EAST ANATOLIA

The mountainous regions, with fertile plateaux where durable yarn is produced, are excellent areas for the making of knotted carpets and kilims. In every valley and every town of the region, carpets of various types are manufactured. Carpets for use in the home are loosely knotted. Besides these, high quality and very fine pure wool carpets, also known as Yörük (Nomadic) carpets, are made here.

Preparing to start a new carpet.

KARS

The carpets of this region are very distinctive and popular. Pure wool and vegetal dyes are used in their making. The predominant geometric patterns are of Caucassian origin.

They are manufactured in a limited range of standard sizes.

Kars pure wool carpet.

Kars pure wool ''Karyola'' carpets.

Kars pure wool ''Kelle'' carpet.

Kars pure wool "Seccade" carpets.

Kars pure wool "Karyola" carpet.

CARPET

BAZAAR 54 İSTANBUL
Nuruosmaniye Cad. No.54,Cağaloğlu
Tel: 90-212 511 21 50 (11 lines)
BAZAAR 54 GALLERİA-İSTANBUL
Ataköy Turizm Merkezi Sahil Yolu
Tel: 90-212 559 03 19
BAZAAR 54 ASPENDOS
Küçükbelkız Köyü, Serik-ANTALYA
Tel: 90-242 735 72 75 (5 lines)

BAZAAR 54 TAVAS
Cankurtaran Mevkii,Tavas-DENİZLİ
90-258 637 42 38 (8 lines)
BAZAAR 54 KAPADOKYA
Zelve Yolu, 50500, Avanos-NEVŞEHİR
Tel: 90-384 511 24 54 (4 lines)
BAZAAR 54 SULTANKÖY
Çamlık, Selçuk-İZMİR
Tel: 90-232 894 80 80 (4 lines)

BAZAAR 54 KUŞADASI
Öküz Mehmet Paşa Kervansarayı
Tel: 90-256 614 34 11
BAZAAR 54 MARMARİS
Yat Limanı, Marina No.1
Tel: 90-252 412 27 83
BAZAAR 54 ANTALYA
Yat Limanı, Kaleiçi No.4
Tel: 90-242 241 02 90

Bazaar 54 is an establishment of **NET GROUP** of **COMPANIES**

PUBLICATION LIST

TURKEY (BN) *(In English, French, German, Italian, Spanish, Dutch)*
ANCIENT CIVILIZATIONS AND RUINS OF TURKEY *(In English)*
ISTANBUL (B) *(In English, French, German, Italian, Spanish, Japanese)*
ISTANBUL (ORT) *(In English, French, German, Italian, Spanish)*
ISTANBUL (BN) *(In English, French, German, Italian, Spanish, Japanese)*
MAJESTIC ISTANBUL *(In English, German)*
TURKISH CARPETS *(In English, French, German, Italian, Spanish, Japanese)*
TURKISH CARPETS *(In English, German)*
THE TOPKAPI PALACE *(In English, French, German, Italian, Italian, Spanish, Japanese, Turkish)*
HAGIA SOPHIA *(In English, French, German, Italian, Spanish)*
THE KARİYE MUSEUM *(In English, French, German, Italian, Spanish)*
ANKARA *(In English, French, German, Italian, Spanish, Turkish)*
Unique CAPPADOCIA *(In English, French, German, Italian, Spanish, Japanese, Turkish)*
CAPPADOCIA (BN) *(In English, French, German, Italian, Spanish, Dutch, Turkish)*
EPHESUS *(In English, French, German, Italian, Spanish, Japanese)*
EPHESUS (BN) *(In English, French, German, Italian, Spanish, Dutch)*
APHRODISIAS *(In English, French, German, Italian, Spanish, Turkish)*
THE TURQUOISE COAST OF TURKEY *(In English)*
PAMUKKALE (HIERAPOLIS) *(In English, French, German, Italian, Spanish, Dutch, Japanese, Turkish)*
PAMUKKALE (BN) *(In English, French, German, Italian, Spanish)*
PERGAMON *(In English, French, German, Italian, Spanish, Japanese)*
LYCIA (AT) *(In English, French, German)*
KARIA (AT) *(In English, French, German)*
ANTALYA (BN) *(In English, French, German, Italian, Dutch, Turkish)*
PERGE *(In English, French, German)*
ASPENDOS *(In English, French, German)*
ALANYA *(In English, French, German, Turkish)*
The Capital of Urartu: VAN *(In English, French, German)*
TRABZON *(In English, French, German, Turkish)*
TURKISH COOKERY *(In English, French, German, Italian, Spanish, Dutch, Japanese, Turkish)*
NASREDDİN HODJA *(In English, French, German, Italian, Spanish, Japanese)*
TÜRKÇE-JAPONCA KONUŞMA KILAVUZU *(Japanese-Turkish)*
ANADOLU UYGARLIKLARI *(Turkish)*

MAPS

TURKEY (NET), TURKEY (ESR), TURKEY (WEST)
TURKEY (SOUTH WEST), ISTANBUL, MARMARİS, ANTALYA-ALANYA, ANKARA, İZMİR, CAPPADOCIA

NET® BOOKSTORES

ISTANBUL
Galleria Ataköy, Sahil Yolu, 34710 Ataköy - Tel: (9-1) 559 09 50
Ramada Hotel, Ordu Caddesi, 226, 34470 Laleli - Tel: (9-1) 513 64 31
İZMİR
Cumhuriyet Bulvarı, 142/B, 35210 Alsancak - Tel: (9-51) 21 26 32

TOUTE LA TURQUIE
KAPPADOKIEN
PERGAMON
HAGIA SOPHIA
C H O R A (THE KARİYE MUSEUM)
NASREDDİN HOCA
LE PALAIS DE TOPKAPI
ANTALYA
TURKISH CARPETS
PAMUKKALE (HIERAPOLIS)
EPHESUS
EDICIÓN ESPAÑOLA — CAPADOCIA
DEUTSCHE AUSGABE — GANZ TÜRKEI
PERGAMON
HAGIA SOPHIA
ISTANBUL
PAMUKKALE (IERAPOLI)
ENGLISH EDITION — CAPPADOCIA
PAMUKKALE (HIERAPOLIS)
ASPENDOS
THE TOPKAPI PALACE
ÉFESO
NASREDDİN HOGIA
PERGE
LYKIEN
LA COCINA TURCA
SAINTE SOPHIE
PERGE
EDICIÓN ESPAÑOLA — ESTAMBUL
PAMUKKALE (HIERAPOLIS)
EL PALACIO DE TOPKAPI
EPHESE
HAGIA SOPHIA
LYCIA
PERGAMO
LA CUISINE TURQUE
TURKISH COOKERY
DEUTSCHE AUSGABE — ISTANBUL
PERGAMON
APHRODISIAS
IL PALAZZO DI TOPKAPI
EDIZIONE ITALIANA — TUTTA LA TURCHIA
ENGLISH EDITION — ISTANBUL
EDITION FRANÇAISE — ANTALYA
PERGAME
NASREDDİN HODJA
ALFOMBRAS TURCAS
C H O R A (LE MUSÉE DE KARİYE)
ASPENDOS
EPHESOS
SANTA SOFIA
PAMUKKALE (HIERAPOLIS)
NASREDDİN HODSCHA
APHRODISIAS
TÜRKISCHE TEPPICHE
C H O R A (IL MUSEO DI KARİYE)
PERGAME
DER TOPKAPI PALAST
ASPENDOS
ENGLISH EDITION — ANTALYA
PAMUKKALE (HIERAPOLIS)
EFES
DIE TÜRKISCHE KÜCHE
ENGLISH EDITION — ALL OF TURKEY
NASREDDİN HODJA
エフェソス
TAPIS TURCS
APHRODISIAS
SANTA SOFIA
PERGAMON
PERGE
C H O R A (DAS KARİYE MUSEUM)
LYCIE
DIE TÜRKISCHE KÜCHE
CARIA
ANADOLU UYGARLIKLARI • Ord. Prof. Dr. Ekren